Trivia for Seniors: 100 Quizzes That Will Increase Knowledge, Keep The Brain Young, And Reduce Chances of Dementia and Alzheimer's by Learning (Large Print For Seniors)

By: Evan Colbert

Table of Contents

Quiz 1 .... **16**

Quiz 2 .... **17**

Quiz 3 .... **18**

Quiz 4 .... **19**

Quiz 5 .... **20**

Quiz 6 .... **21**

Quiz 7 .... **22**

Quiz 8 .... **23**

Quiz 9 .... **24**

Quiz 10 .... **25**

Quiz 11 .... **26**

Quiz 12 .... **27**

Quiz 13 .... **28**

Quiz 14 .... **29**

Quiz 15 .... **30**

Quiz 16 .... **31**

Quiz 17 .... **32**

Quiz 18 .... **33**

Quiz 19 .... **34**

Quiz 20 .... **35**

Quiz 21 .... **36**

Quiz 22 .... **37**

Quiz 23 .... **38**

Quiz 24 .... **39**

Quiz 25 .... **40**

Quiz 26 .... **41**

Quiz 27 .... **42**

Quiz 28 .... **43**

Quiz 29 .... **44**

Quiz 30 .... **45**

Quiz 31 .... **46**

Quiz 32 .... **47**

Quiz 33 .... **48**

Quiz 34 .... **49**

Quiz 35 .... **50**

Quiz 36 .... **51**

Quiz 37 .... **52**

Quiz 38 .... **53**

Quiz 39 .... **54**

Quiz 40 .... **55**

Quiz 41 .... **56**

Quiz 42 .... **57**

Quiz 43 .... **58**

Quiz 44 .... **59**

Quiz 45 .... **60**

Quiz 46 .... **61**

Quiz 47 .... **62**

Quiz 48 .... **63**

Quiz 49 .... **64**

Quiz 50 ....**65**

Quiz 51 ....**66**

Quiz 52 ....**67**

Quiz 53 ....**68**

Quiz 54 ....**69**

Quiz 55 ....**70**

Quiz 56 ....**71**

Quiz 57 ....**72**

Quiz 58 ....**73**

Quiz 59 ....**74**

Quiz 60 ....**75**

Quiz 61 ....**76**

Quiz 62 ....**77**

Quiz 63 ....**78**

Quiz 64 ....**79**

Quiz 65 ....**80**

Quiz 66 ....**81**

Quiz 67 .... **82**

Quiz 68 .... **83**

Quiz 69 .... **84**

Quiz 70 .... **85**

Quiz 71 .... **86**

Quiz 72 .... **87**

Quiz 73 .... **88**

Quiz 74 .... **89**

Quiz 75 .... **90**

Quiz 76 .... **91**

Quiz 77 .... **92**

Quiz 78 .... **93**

Quiz 79 .... **94**

Quiz 80 .... **95**

Quiz 81 .... **96**

Quiz 82 .... **97**

Quiz 83 .... **98**

Quiz 84 99

Quiz 85 100

Quiz 86 101

Quiz 87 102

Quiz 88 103

Quiz 89 104

Quiz 90 105

Quiz 91 106

Quiz 92 107

Quiz 93 108

Quiz 94 109

Quiz 95 110

Quiz 96 111

Quiz 97 112

Quiz 98 113

Quiz 99 114

Quiz 100 115

Answer Key **116**

Quiz 1 Answers **116**

Quiz 2 Answers **117**

Quiz 3 Answers **118**

Quiz 4 Answers **119**

Quiz 5 Answers **120**

Quiz 6 Answers **121**

Quiz 7 Answers **122**

Quiz 8 Answers **123**

Quiz 9 Answers **124**

Quiz 10 Answers **125**

Quiz 11 Answers **126**

Quiz 12 Answers **127**

Quiz 13 Answers **128**

Quiz 14 Answers **129**

Quiz 15 Answers **130**

Quiz 16 Answers **131**

Quiz 17 Answers 132

Quiz 18 Answers 133

Quiz 19 Answers 134

Quiz 20 Answers 135

Quiz 21 Answers 136

Quiz 22 Answers 137

Quiz 23 Answers 138

Quiz 24 Answers 139

Quiz 25 Answers 140

Quiz 26 Answers 141

Quiz 27 Answers 142

Quiz 28 Answers 143

Quiz 29 Answers 144

Quiz 30 Answers 145

Quiz 31 Answers 146

Quiz 32 Answers 147

Quiz 33 Answers 148

Quiz 34 Answers 149

Quiz 35 Answers 150

Quiz 36 Answers 151

Quiz 37 Answers 152

Quiz 38 Answers 153

Quiz 39 Answers 154

Quiz 40 Answers 155

Quiz 41 Answers 156

Quiz 42 Answers 157

Quiz 43 Answers 158

Quiz 44 Answers 159

Quiz 45 Answers 160

Quiz 46 Answers 161

Quiz 47 Answers 162

Quiz 48 Answers 163

Quiz 49 Answers 164

Quiz 50 Answers 165

Quiz 51 Answers 166

Quiz 52 Answers 167

Quiz 53 Answers 168

Quiz 54 Answers 169

Quiz 55 Answers 170

Quiz 56 Answers 171

Quiz 57 Answers 172

Quiz 58 Answers 173

Quiz 59 Answers 174

Quiz 60 Answers 175

Quiz 61 Answers 176

Quiz 62 Answers 177

Quiz 63 Answers 178

Quiz 64 Answers 179

Quiz 65 Answers 180

Quiz 66 Answers 181

Quiz 67 Answers 182

Quiz 68 Answers **183**

Quiz 69 Answers **184**

Quiz 70 Answers **185**

Quiz 71 Answers **186**

Quiz 72 Answers **187**

Quiz 73 Answers **188**

Quiz 74 Answers **189**

Quiz 75 Answers **190**

Quiz 76 Answers **191**

Quiz 77 Answers **192**

Quiz 78 Answers **193**

Quiz 79 Answers **194**

Quiz 80 Answers **195**

Quiz 81 Answers **196**

Quiz 82 Answers **197**

Quiz 83 Answers **198**

Quiz 85 Answers **200**

Quiz 86 Answers 201

Quiz 87 Answers 202

Quiz 88 Answers 203

Quiz 89 Answers 204

Quiz 90 Answers 205

Quiz 91 Answers 206

Quiz 92 Answers 207

Quiz 93 Answers 208

Quiz 94 Answers 209

Quiz 95 Answers 210

Quiz 96 Answers 211

Quiz 97 Answers 212

Quiz 98 Answers 213

Quiz 99 Answers 214

Quiz 100 Answers 215

Quiz 1

1. This Dickens classic saw Miss Havisham get left at the altar. What novel is it?

2. Who composed the Wedding March?

3. Who invented the TV?

4. What decade was the Halley's Comet last seen?

5. What shoe company did Michael Jordan famously promote?

6. What are the espadrilles?

7. What is the smallest country in the world?

8. What initials did the rapper Hammer lose?

9. Who invented the Olympics as we know it today?

10. Who was the second president of the United States?

Quiz 2

1. What is the other name for a prune?

2. Louis Daguerre developed what art medium?

3. What is the movie title of Disney's Rapunzel?

4. This monster was created by a famous doctor. What is its name?

5. What is the name of the bear in The Jungle Book?

6. What is the square root of 81?

7. Wreck-It Ralph has a go-kart racing game. Is it called Rush, Slam Rush, or Sugar Rush?

8. What is the other name for a female dog?

9. Who is the patron saint of Ireland?

10. Name the Shakespearean play wherein this quote came from: *The course of true love never did run smooth.*

Quiz 3

1. Who is the author of the Grapes of Wrath?

2. How many valves does a trumpet have?

3. What is Dick Grayson better recognized as?

4. James Bond was first played by Roger Moore in what film?

5. The Eurasian Tawny (or Brown Owl) makes this distinctive call. It sounds like too-wit, too-wu. Which gender makes the call? Male birds, Female birds, Both, Males make the former sound, Females make the latter.

6. How many sides does a standard pencil have?

7. Who was recognized as the Welsh Wizard?

8. Who is the British ice skater who won gold at the Lake Placid Olympics?

9. What powers the sun?

10. *Hit and Miss* was the theme song of what TV show?

Quiz 4

1. Liverpool lies on what river?

2. What do you call the small indentations on a golf ball?

3. What do you call a white knee-length pleated skirt in the traditional Greek dress?

4. Who is the British actor in the American TV series House?

5. The Titanic sunk in this year.

6. Who is Shrek's wife?

7. What is the other name for fish eggs?

8. King Arthur was born in what Cornish village?

9. English law banned this traditional Scottish musical instrument. What is it?

10. What is the other name for a young hen?

Quiz 5

1. Who assassinated Yigal Amir in 1995?

2. Manhattan, Brooklyn, and the Bronx are a part of what U.S. city?

3. What is the country of the soccer player, Wayne Rooney?

4. Who starred in *The Missionary*?

5. The Greek god Hermes is akin to what Roman god?

6. What is the largest living structure on Earth?

7. The Palace of Versailles is closest to what European city?

8. Tony Stark is the alias of what superhero?

9. Who is the father of the modern Italy?

10. Michael Jordan switched to what sport in 1993?

Quiz 6

1. What is Norma Jean Baker more commonly known?

2. The definition of clandestine is: noisy, secret or orange?

3. If you walked on a flat surface in a straight line, could you end up walking in circles eventually?

4. The Diamond State is the nickname of what U.S. state?

5. *La Gioconda* more commonly goes by this name.

6. What is the rarest blood type in humans?

7. What word describes a number system with a base of two?

8. What item does Dewey Decimal System?

9. What is a burette?

10. What trees lose their leaves in winter?

Quiz 7

1. What village was near the house in Noel Edmund's House Party?

2. This city is known for its leaning tower. What is its name?

3. This sort of doctor can help get your braces. What doctor is it?

4. The Statue of Liberty carries the torch in which hand?

5. What country gave the USA the Statue of Liberty?

6. This nation's soldiers wear white kilts.

7. Who is the music group in the 70s with the hit single *Shadow Dancing?*

8. How long does a human red blood cell live?

9. What is the main bonding ingredient in tempera paint's color pigments?

10. How many legs do butterflies have?

Quiz 8

1. What is the medical term for low blood sugar?

2. What chess piece can only move diagonally?

3. What is the name of the inventor of the safety pin?

4. The name of the protagonist in *Hunger Games* is?

5. True or false: Is the color scarlet a deep red?

6. Can you lick your elbow?

7. What is the brand of the car featured in the 80s *Back To The Future?*

8. The word "crouton" only has one anagram. What is it?

9. What are sheep if cats are feline?

10. What planet has a ring?

Quiz 9

1. Who invented the rabies vaccination?

2. Who is the Dickens' character that said "Expecting something to turn up?"

3. How many books are there in the New Testament?

4. Wine gives off a scent and has a specific name for the odor. What is it?

5. What is the name of the fairy in Peter Pan?

6. "I am the president of United States and I am not going to eat any more broccoli," are the famous words uttered by whom?

7. How many strings does a cello have?

8. What Football Club plays home matches at Home Park?

9. Who has more hair follicles, blondes or brunettes?

10. What movement was founded by L. Ron Hubbard?

Quiz 10

1. What food do Giant Pandas normally eat?

2. Who owns Microsoft?

3. Who are the four Masters of High Renaissance?

4. How many months have exactly 30 days?

5. What is the world's largest diamond producing country?

6. What is the Judicial Branch?

7. What is the other name for a male bovine (cattle, oxen, buffaloes, etc.)?

8. What oronymic word is defined as murder and as the mirth of a male?

9. Who wrote about the Cornish mermaids mentioned in the children's books?

10. What is the name of the Library of the University of Oxford?

Quiz 11

1. What is the capital of the United States?

2. Who is the inventor of the light Bulb?

3. What are the first organisms to grow back after the fire?

4. On what everyday item would you find the inscription Decus Et Tutamen?

5. Where did Xmas, a term that means Christmas, came from? Greek X for Christ; X for kisses; an early typographical error in bibles; or, secularization?

6. What is the name of Nemo's dad in *Finding Nemo*?

7. Who is the guitarist recognized as Slowhand?

8. What is the nickname for finding treasures at junk shops and garage sales?

9. What is the TV's *The Saint*'s character name*?*

10. What did Sir Christopher Cockerell invent?

Quiz 12

1. What is the largest producer of tin in the world?

2. What is the name of the dog in the Punch and Judy Show?

3. In what month does the Kentucky Derby take place?

4. How many borders does the Gulf of Mexico touch in the American states?

5. What is rum distilled from?

6. Who invented the jet engine?

7. Who composed the Minute Waltz?

8. How many is a "Baker's Dozen"?

9. Who married (the animated character) Princess Fiona?

10. Who is the primary producer of newsprint in the world?

Quiz 13

1. What country did reggae music originate?

2. *Brown-Eyed Handsome Man* was a posthumous hit for which singer?

3. What is the nickname of the clock at the Palace of Westminster in London?

4. What is the medical term for stroke?

5. What is the nickname of a Mountain Ash tree?

6. Martina Navratilova has been on the winning side in the Federation Cup for what two countries?

7. This character picked a peck of pickled peppers.

8. Who is the male singer from Salford who is called The Voice?

9. What is the height of a double elephant folio book?

10. David Kotkin magically changed his name to what famous magician?

Quiz 14

1. Hug a guling. You are now hugging: a toy, a creature, or a pillow?

2. To convert graphite into a diamond, you need this pressure and temperature.

3. A Benedictine monk invented champagne. What is his name?

4. What animal's name translates as water horse?

5. What is the other name for a baby deer?

6. What European city is recognized as the Balti Capital?

7. What national park features Coniston Water?

8. What famous brand of horror films is home to Bray Studios?

9. The Dome of the Rock is found in what city?

10. What is the most famous painting by Pablo Picasso?

Quiz 15

1. Who invented the telephone?

2. How far is the moon from the earth?

3. What is the square root of 144?

4. What is the average temperature of the human body in Celsius?

5. What do you call the plants and animals that live on the floor of the lake?

6. What article of clothing was called after the Scottish inventor?

7. What is the Land of Morning Calm?

8. What is a trepanning?

9. What is an otter's home called?

10. If you had pogonophobia, what would you be afraid of?

Quiz 16

1. Who is the remaining living member of the Beatles?

2. What is the largest library in the world?

3. Who is the singer that has a hit song, *Let's Go To San Francisco?*

4. How many bases are in a diamond (sports)?

5. What action burns more calories, sleeping or watching TV?

6. What color and creature prefixes the names of the following five nouns: bill, hammer, legs, throat, and head (two answers the color and the creature)?

7. What do the letters HB stand for on a pencil?

8. The UK TV show that is most watched of all time is?

9. Mount Everest was called after this knighted explorer.

10. What country first used the paper money?

Quiz 17

1. What chess piece moves in an L-shape?

2. What Jewish festival is recognized as the Festival of Lights?

3. What is the name of the Australian toy that returns to you after thrown?

4. The year LEGO was founded: 1942, 1932, or 1952?

5. What is the other name for a baby fish?

6. What does a manometer measure?

7. What is the other name for a female deer?

8. The prefix tacho regards: Speed, Time, Weight, or Light?

9. What is the third major Balearic Island?

10. What is the Bill of Rights?

Quiz 18

1. What number does "giga" stand for?

2. On an Indian restaurant menu, how is a potato known?

3. "Master of the ivory keys" means you play what?

4. What disease is the focus of oncology?

5. Presbyopia affects what organ?

6. On what river does the City of Leeds stand?

7. Who invented the Polaroid camera?

8. How long does the light from the sun take to reach the earth?

9. What is the square root of one-fourth?

10. Liverpool, Everton, Manchester City, and Manchester United were played only by this player.

Quiz 19

1. Who is the first female president of the state in Latin America?

2. What is the area where baseball players wait?

3. What is the name of King Arthur's mum?

4. Who is the founder of Facebook?

5. In the charity AHA, what does H stand for?

6. Who is the leader that died in St. Helena?

7. How old is the earth?

8. What is the average body temperature of a human in Fahrenheit?

9. The oldest known fossil is made up of what sort of organism?

10. What is the international soccer competition held every four years?

Quiz 20

1. What does Columbus originally expected to find?

2. What uses needles inserted into the body at specific points for healing?

3. What of these is not like the others?

4. What are a palmiped's feet?

5. The Scoville Heat Unit Scale measures what?

6. What months have 30 days?

7. Hamilton Smith invented this household item in 1858.

8. Rugby's Jonah Lomu plays for this nation.

9. What is known as the Earth's oldest living thing?

10. Who invented the first battery?

Quiz 21

1. Name the 7 continents.

2. How many days are there in a fortnight?

3. The teddy bear was called after what famous person?

4. The United States' 16th president is?

5. Pharaoh was a ruler of which ancient civilization?

6. What are the three primary colors?

7. What life-saving device did Sir Humphry Davy invent?

8. Is a tomato a fruit or vegetable?

9. What is Superman's nickname?

10. What is designed and driven by George Stephenson?

Quiz 22

1. What artist was called Jack the Dripper?

2. Who is the artist who originally sang *Don't Go Breaking My Heart* with Elton John?

3. What is the footwear invented in 1815 that enables the wearer to move quickly over flat, smooth surfaces?

4. The trilogy of the Lord of the Rings is directed by?

5. What is the top color of a rainbow?

6. What did the crocodile swallow in Peter Pan?

7. What are the only two countries to have a border with the US?

8. What is the other name for a baby rooster?

9. What is the Fibonacci sequence?

10. Who is this Russian dancer that changed ballet in the modern era?

Quiz 23

1. How many innings are there in a baseball game?

2. What name do a planet and a mollusk share?

3. What is the color of the Smurfs?

4. How many U.S. cents are there in a dime?

5. The oldest forest is found where?

6. "Snap, crackle, and pop" what cereal is this called?

7. What mammal lays eggs?

8. What is a Pyrogen?

9. In the Peanuts cartoon strip, what was the surname of Lucy and Linus?

10. Scott Hamilton won Olympic gold for the USA on what sport?

Quiz 24

1. What is the soccer player who can use his hands?

2. Greyfriar's School best pupil (in literature)?

3. What city is called the City of Angels?

4. What is the character created by the author of Tracy Beaker children's book?

5. What is a baby goat called?

6. Who invented Kodak cameras?

7. What is the sun made out of?

8. What is the bull's eye color on the archery target?

9. What measures the acidity or alkalinity?

10. Who is the author of the Father Brown detective novels?

Quiz 25

1. What is the touchdown's point in U.S. football?

2. How many years are there in a millennium?

3. Ten-pin bowling's perfect score is?

4. What mythological beast has a lion's body and an eagle's wings and head?

5. What measure of energy comes from the Latin word meaning "heat"?

6. A package of hotdog buns contains how many pieces?

7. What coin introduced by Henry VII had gold and longevity?

8. Who is the reggae-singing star who died on the 11th of May, 1981?

9. Tesla units apply to what? Magnetism or Sound?

10. What do leukemia sufferers have too many of?

Quiz 26

1. Who is the Playwright who wrote The Seagull?

2. What is the cause of the color fever discovered in 1900?

3. What is the bluebird a symbol of?

4. How many lines should a limerick have?

5. What fictional character lived at 221b Baker Street?

6. Pandora Braithwaite was the girlfriend of what eponymous literary character?

7. Who is the person that won the Wimbledon singles in 1998 after twice losing in the final?

8. The Himalayan poppy's color is?

9. You can play a game on a crown green. What game is it?

10. What trains travel from St. Pancras Station to "the Continent"?

Quiz 27

1. What car company makes the Celica?

2. What is the other name for a male swan?

3. What is Mozart's full baptismal name?

4. What is the equivalent of Neptune in the Greek mythology?

5. What is the other name for a female goat?

6. Emerald is the birthstone for what month?

7. What is the meaning of the Greek prefix—geo?

8. What is the name of the pointer on a Sun Dial?

9. What is the total of the ten consecutive prime numbers beginning from 13?

10. What is 2 cubed?

Quiz 28

1. What kind of sports spikes and blocks?

2. What country hosted the Formula 1 race for the first time in 2011?

3. Who is the author of orcs, hobbits, and elves?

4. Who is the winner of six Wimbledon single titles in the 80s?

5. In what state is the Grand Canyon located?

6. Name the biggest freshwater lake in the world.

7. Who is the youngest president of the USA?

8. How many months have exactly 30 days?

9. What is a Cerberus?

10. What two numbers are used in a binary code?

Quiz 29

1. In what year was the Piper Alpha disaster?

2. This nation sent an Armada to attack Britain in 1588.

3. Saint Patrick is the Patron Saint of what country?

4. What color is a Welsh poppy?

5. What big country is closest to New Zealand?

6. What is the other name for a baby fox?

7. What is the other name for a group of cattle?

8. What do you call a horse's shoes?

9. Thirsty people need ...?

10. Major League Baseball's first African-American player is?

Quiz 30

1. What is the TV program that has regular presenters namely Trevor McDonald, Carol Barnes, Sandy Gall, Reginald Bosanquet, Alastair Burnett, and Alastair Stewart?

2. What is mainland Britain's southernmost point located in Cornwall?

3. What is the other name for a baby butterfly?

4. What is the planet that is seventh from the sun?

5. What is the film where Humphrey Bogart said, "We'll always have Paris?"

6. Whose person's face is on a dime?

7. The supply of sugar between the muscles and blood is controlled by which hormone?

8. Who are the members of the Legislative Branch?

9. What country will you see looking over the sea from The White Cliffs of Dover?

10. What planet spins the fastest?

Quiz 31

1. What letter represents 5 in the Roman numerals?

2. What is the largest city in Wales?

3. What James Bond villain did Donald Pleasance, Max Von Sydow, Telly Savalas, and Charles Gray played?

4. What is Ping-pong originally called?

5. What state is called the Lone Star State?

6. Jamie Lee Curtis is the dad of?

7. Human skin makes up most of the dust in your home: T/F?

8. What percentage of our body weight is water?

9. Name the 5 great lakes.

10. Who discovered the rubber?

Quiz 32

1. What order of monks is recognized as Blackfriars?

2. What is the postal abbreviation for Idaho?

3. The names of Snow White's seven dwarfs are?

4. What body of water separates France and England?

5. Who are the protagonists in Watership Down?

6. What temperature does water boil at?

7. What is the other name for a baby bird?

8. What is this illness that killed thousands across Europe during the 14th Century?

9. The horse is the fastest land animal: T/F

10. The year MDCCXIV is how many years off from 2014?

Quiz 33

1. What year does the euro been introduced as a legal currency?

2. Who is the king that was killed at the Battle of Camelford?

3. Mozzarella Cheese is made from the milk of what animal?

4. How many states are there in the United States of America?

5. Prince Andrew's birth year is?

6. On a farm, a kid is a baby what?

7. Who composed "Clair de Lune?"

8. This cartoon's best buddy is Barney and his wife is Wilma.

9. Who is the *Vampire Chronicles'* author?

10. Who is the TV character that always says, "Live long and prosper?"

Quiz 34

1. What is Cinderella's coach made from?

2. Who founded the Lotus Cars?

3. What is the infant whale commonly called?

4. What process involves heating an ore to obtain a metal?

5. What is the biggest delta in the world?

6. The Mau Mau uprising (1952-60) took place in what country?

7. What is the very first women's magazine called?

8. In golf, a birdie is 1 under par, an eagle is 2 under, what is three under par called?

9. What is the moon's distance from the Earth?

10. The Fresh Prince of where was the subject of a sitcom of 140+ shows?

Quiz 35

1. What is the National flower of China?

2. What is the name of King Arthur's sword?

3. What 1815 battle in Belgium marked the final defeat of Napoleon?

4. His nose grew when he tells a lie.

5. What fingernail grows fastest?

6. Where did Billy Butlin open his first holiday camp?

7. Tour De France's winners' jersey color?

8. How many patents did Thomas Edison file?

9. What are the Munroes?

10. What is the other name for a female ship?

Quiz 36

1. What is the diameter of the Earth?

2. What is the other name for a male falcon?

3. What is the other name for a male turkey?

4. What superhero owns Stark Industries?

5. What nation produces ⅔ of the world's vanilla?

6. Who is the Italian astronomer who invented the thermometer in 1592?

7. What is Captain Mainwaring's first name in TV show Dad's Army?

8. What is the other name for a male goose?

9. What kind of weapon is a falchion?

10. What country's flag is the only one that features the map of the country on it?

Quiz 37

1. John Bonham, who died at the aged of 32, was the former drummer of what rock band?

2. Where is Mulhacen?

3. Who is the leader of the British National Party?

4. Who threw herself under King George V's horse in 1913?

5. What percentage of an egg's weight is the shell?

6. Who is the English king who had six wives?

7. In what state did both Kennedy and Johnson die?

8. Which 50s classic TV show featured the characters Charlie Allnut and Rosie Sayer?

9. What age will the horse be if it becomes a mare?

10. *They Called The Wind Mariah* is featured in what musical?

Quiz 38

1. What is the other name for a male sheep?

2. What metal is heavier, silver or gold?

3. What is the Land of White Elephant?

4. Which of the planets in our solar system is closest to the sun?

5. What is the other name for a female horse?

6. What is the only mammal that can't jump?

7. Who is buried in Grants tomb?

8. The Cresta Run is found in which country?

9. The Giants, in baseball, came from?

10. What does "coyote" mean? Wild, crazy, or trickster?

Quiz 39

1. In what Disney movie is there a man called Gaston?

2. How long in meters is the thread of a silkworm?

3. What name is given to a courtyard in a castle or the wall surrounding the outer court of a castle?

4. By what title was the Spanish dictator, General Franco, known?

5. A cow is sold for five magic beans by whom?

6. Which famous historical document begins *with "When in the course of human events...?"*

7. What is the other name for a baby snake?

8. Cut a rabbit and marinate it in juniper berries and wine and then stew. This is the recipe for?

9. What is the river between Scotland and England?

10. What is the other name for a male dog?

Quiz 40

1. What is a Manticore?

2. What is the world's fastest land animal?

3. What is the first element on the periodic table of elements?

4. What is the other name for a baby eagle?

5. What do you call a timespan of one thousand years?

6. Who was called The Divine Ponytail in football?

7. How many UK households currently watch TV in black & white? 130, 1300 or 13,000?

8. The Eiffel tower was built by?

9. What famous battle was fought on St. Crispin's day?

10. Yuma, AZ is the world's most _____ city: Sunny, Hot, Humid or Dry?

Quiz 41

1. What is the R in the United Nation's UNHCR?

2. Name all four of the Marx Brothers.

3. Who composed the music for the ballets Sleeping Beauty and Swan Lake?

4. Who is the author of Dr. No and Thunderball?

5. What kind of animal is Baloo in *Jungle Book*?

6. When was William Shakespeare born?

7. What is an e-book?

8. The national flower of Italy is?

9. What is the other name for a baby sheep?

10. Long Island holds what kind of Triple Crown Race in horse racing?

Quiz 42

1. Who is the first Republican president of America?

2. The buttons on a women's blouse are located on what side?

3. The name of the three tunnels in *The Great Escape* are?

4. The US state of Georgia is famous for what fruit?

5. Who is the CEO of the company, Google?

6. What does SLR stand for as found in a camera?

7. How many milligrams make a gram?

8. A test match in cricket can be played where?

9. What BBC series about collectibles began in 1979?

10. What is the capital of Hawaii?

Quiz 43

1. If you go into space, do you get taller?

2. What sort of animal did St. George slay?

3. This city lies across the bay from San Francisco.

4. If you boil water, you get?

5. What does a numismatist study or collect?

6. Triskaidekaphobia is the fear of what?

7. The Parks Movement was led by which English town?

8. Who captained Jules Verne's submarine Nautilus?

9. What American state harvests the most potatoes?

10. How old is the sun?

Quiz 44

1. How many sides does a triangle have?

2. Who is the father of the English throne's 16th in line?

3. How many colors are there in a rainbow?

4. Who is younger, Serena or Venus Williams?

5. What is the City of Canals?

6. Who is the patron saint of doctors?

7. Who is the fictional detective that lived at 221b Baker Street?

8. How many wives did Henry VIII have?

9. The first recyclable plastic bottle was launch by Coca-Cola in what year?

10. The US flag has how many white stripes?

Quiz 45

1. What is the capital of England?

2. What is the full name of the IRS?

3. What is the name of the annual open golf tournament of the U.S.?

4. A Lafite-Rothschild is a type of?

5. What animal has a leopard and camel cross-breed?

6. What amendment limited the number of terms a president could serve after Franklin D. Roosevelt?

7. What is Mickey Mouse's original name?

8. The universe's strongest known magnet is?

9. Name the three primary colors.

10. Who improved the care for wounded soldiers during the Victoria era (nurse)?

Quiz 46

1. Who is the first gymnast that received a 10 at the Olympics?

2. Who is the carmaker of the Fiesta, Ka, and Mondeo?

3. Fried tarantulas are still a delicacy in some cultures: T/F?

4. What do doctors look at an eye through?

5. Who is the longest reigning British Monarch?

6. The Walker Cup is competed for in what sport?

7. When did William Shakespeare die?

8. What is the name of Peppa Pig's brother?

9. What is the Executive Branch?

10. What is the name of the dog in "Blue Peter"?

Quiz 47

1. Who is the actor in Moby Dick in 1956 that had a wooden leg?

2. What is the lowest point on Earth?

3. Rome, Italy has never hosted the Summer Olympic Games: T/F?

4. What is the first commercially manufactured breakfast cereal?

5. What is the flute family's smallest member?

6. The Canary Islands get their name from which animal?

7. What is the tallest mountain on Earth?

8. Where did the First Industrial Revolution take place?

9. How many days are there in a leap year?

10. The US declared war on what country after the bombing of Pearl Harbor?

Quiz 48

1. What bone lies between the knee and the hips?

2. What is an antonym?

3. 3 consecutive strikes in bowling in the last frame are called what?

4. When did the First World War start?

5. In publishing, what does POD mean?

6. Vision changes as you get older. Why?

7. Where is the Judicial Branch located?

8. What is the groundnut better recognized as?

9. What two letters are both symbols for 1,000?

10. Only one sort of space rock survives impact with the Earth's surface. What is its name?

Quiz 49

1. What Shakespeare play features Shylock?

2. Flying from New York City to London crosses which ocean?

3. The South American city of Brazillia is built in the shape of what?

4. What war took place from 1939 to 1945?

5. What is the other name for a baby frog?

6. What is the top stripe on the US flag, white or red?

7. The Greek God of music goes by this name.

8. The two families in Romeo and Juliet are?

9. How many periods does a hockey game have?

10. What plant has the scientific name Galanthus?

Quiz 50

1. What is the year Alaska was sold to the U.S?

2. How many petals does the Tudor Rose have?

3. What color is a panda?

4. At room temperature, what metal is not solid?

5. What is Sir Isaac Newton's fruit of gravity?

6. What sporting legend is recognized as The Golden Bear?

7. Where is the Executive Branch located?

8. Who is Peter Parker's secret identity?

9. What is the herb used as the main ingredient of Pesto sauce?

10.   What year did the Spanish Civil War end?

Quiz 51

1. What country has the highest population density?

2. Bram Stoker used this historical prince in his famous Dracula novel.

3. What color is associated with the breast cancer charity?

4. What is the use of tarot cards?

5. The U.S. President and the Vice President are officially elected by which person?

6. Bowling term for knocking down the remaining pins after your first bowl during a frame?

7. What is the address of the White House?

8. Who is the singer in the 1985 *Saving All My Love For You?*"

9. The world's deadliest snake is?

10. Name the four main human blood groups.

Quiz 52

1. What is the highest mountain in Africa?

2. Where did the Olympic Games originate?

3. Where did the pineapple plant originate?

4. How many sides does a dodecagon have?

5. What fingernail grows the fastest?

6. Who is the heavyweight boxing champ with 49 undefeated fights?

7. What bird has the largest wingspan?

8. What is allspice alternatively recognized as?

9. What is the solar system's largest satellite?

10. What does the atomic number of an element indicate about its nucleus?

Quiz 53

1. What is the name of Helen of Troy's husband?

2. How many players make up a basketball team?

3. The designer of Millennium Dome is?

4. The Myristica Fragrams tree provides two spices. One is mace. What is the other?

5. What is the longest highway in the world?

6. According to the Christian Bible, how many forms of God exist?

7. This societal faux pas was banned from street signs by Cambridge City Council in 2014: Finger pointing. Abbreviations. Apostrophes. Oxford comma?

8. Does Nitroglycerine treat cardiac arrests: T/F?

9. What is the most malleable metal?

10. What is the name of the first woman member of the Parliament in Britain?

Quiz 54

1. What is the other name for a female bovine?

2. Biblion is a Greek word which was used to give the bible its name. What does this Greek word mean?

3. What is the best known artificial international language?

4. Bees make what sweetener?

5. What is the Law of Conservation of Energy?

6. Princess Aurora is a character of what Disney hit?

7. Nigel Starmer Smith is a name most famously associated with what sport?

8. An angon, used by Anglo-Saxons, is what? A weapon, a fruit, or a vase?

9. *Snot Rap* was a top 10 hit in England by which DJ?

10. What is the largest coffee growing country?

Quiz 55

1. Who is this famous Italian painter who painted Sir Galahad and Sir Percival's sister's death into oil?

2. What is a baby kangaroo called?

3. Australia was discovered by whom?

4. Where are half of the world's one hundred highest bridges located?

5. What is the other name for an insect poop?

6. Who plays against the USA in golf's Walker Cup?

7. Where in your body is your patella?

8. If you freeze water, you get ...?

9. The first female DJ of Radio 1 is?

10. What is the NBA's nickname for championship series that determine best in the league?

Quiz 56

1. What bird was domesticated first?

2. A triangle has how many sides?

3. Maria Montessori was a famous name in what field?

4. What is kaolin also recognized as?

5. Red Stripe Lager was originally produced in what country?

6. Who wrote Julius Caesar, Macbeth, and Hamlet?

7. How many tentacles does a squid have?

8. What is the other name for a male bird?

9. What is the country known for Land of the Midnight Sun?

10. Is the number of neck vertebrae in a giraffe the same as the human?

Quiz 57

1. What does Fred Flintstone wear around his neck?

2. What is the world's highest mountain?

3. Where does Greg Norman come from?

4. Where are the Pyrenees?

5. Dublin is situated at the mouth of what river?

6. Sleepy, Doc, Dopey, Happy, Grumpy, Sneezy. Who's missing?

7. In what year did Foinavon win the Grand National?

8. Who was the first person to see Jesus after his resurrection?

9. What is Che Guevara's nationality?

10. Where is the Legislative Branch located?

Quiz 58

1. You think you are experiencing something that has happened before exactly as it is now. "I'm having a case of _____!"

2. The Battle of Culloden took place on what year?

3. A group of lions is better known as a _____.

4. What star other than the sun is closest to the earth?

5. The Last Judgement was the first painting of whose Italian painter?

6. What is the most widely eaten fish in the world?

7. What is the other name for a male duck?

8. What is the most widely spoken language in Brazil?

9. What is the other name for a baby goose?

10. Who is the actress that had her career launched with a series of Campari commercials?

Quiz 59

1. In what year was the Queen Mother born?

2. What state is called the Aloha State?

3. Where is the Suez Canal?

4. What is the other name for a male deer?

5. What is Lady Penelope's chauffeur name in "Thunderbirds"?

6. In what 20th-century decade was Barbie's boyfriend Ken first made?

7. What is a secure case that holds and displays decanters?

8. The Cathedral Church of St. Michael is located where?

9. What organization has the motto "Nation shall speak peace unto nation?"

10. How many holes are there on a golf course?

Quiz 60

1. If you were eating du Barry, what would you be eating?

2. Barack Obama is the ____th president of the U.S.?

3. Who is the pet owl of Harry Potter?

4. Who painted the Mona Lisa?

5. The Titanic sunk in which year?

6. What is the opposite of matter?

7. What are sweetbreads?

8. How many cups are in a gallon?

9. What did the Emancipation Proclamation declare?

10. What is the state in the US that begins with letter P?

Quiz 61

1. What country was home to the Moa bird that became extinct about 500 years ago?

2. How many pockets does a snooker table have?

3. The conductor Sir Henry Joseph Wood established what legendary music festival in 1895?

4. What is the common name of a Black Leopard?

5. Ice cream on a sponge and topped with meringue are the elements of what classic pudding dish?

6. Who lived at 221B, Baker Street, London?

7. Tired people need what?

8. What is the shortest month of the year?

9. What is the black box's color?

10. Stellar winds can only be found on what kind of terrain?

Quiz 62

1. How many pounds of saffron require how many crocus flowers?

2. How many sides does a stop sign have?

3. The Great Pyramid of Giza resides in what country?

4. What is the busiest city airport for international passengers in 2014 that beat out Heathrow?

5. What is the first organ that is successfully transplanted from a corpse to a live person?

6. What is the other name for a baby swan?

7. Which Vitamin goes by Ascorbic Acid?

8. What do deciduous trees do?

9. Excel, part of the Microsoft Office suite, is what type of software?

10. What is a Kraken?

Quiz 63

1. What is John Wayne's original name?

2. What family of animals do llamas belong?

3. Incandescent light bulbs got a revamp by whose inventor?

4. June has how many days?

5. Sherlock's Dr. Watson's first name?

6. Who is *The Quiet Man* actor who was in 142 films?

7. Jewish tradition of Yahrzeit is a type of _____. (Protein, Season, Yahrzeit, or Game)

8. What is the name of the monk in the Robin Hood legend?

9. What is the name of the cowboy in Toy Story?

10. What is Frodo's last name?

Quiz 64

1. Anna Sewell wrote which children's classic book?

2. In geometry, what name is given to a triangle with three different sides?

3. Who is the author of *Death in Venice*?

4. What does the Latin phrase caveat emptor mean?

5. What is the world's most well-known green vegetable?

6. How many rings does the Olympic flag have?

7. What American newspaper first exposed the Watergate Scandal?

8. What is a circus tent's name?

9. What is the Robert the Bruce battle where he defeated English forces in 1314?

10. Andrew Carnegie made his fortune in what industry?

Quiz 65

1. What is the biggest desert in the world?

2. Who is the first woman Prime Minister of Britain?

3. What BBC music program ran from 1964 – 2006?

4. Is a white gold ring made of pure gold?

5. A radioactive source is measured by what unit?

6. A witch flies on a _____.

7. The term pulmonary relates to what organ?

8. This is the only U.S. state that does not follow the Daylight Savings Time.

9. What is the other name for a young bovine?

10. How old is the universe?

Quiz 66

1. How many "Great Lakes" are there?

2. In the Bible, who was the wife of King Ahab?

3. Who is the first African-American MLB player?

4. What is Superman's weakness?

5. Where is the Birmingham state?

6. What is the Chinese game with small tiles?

7. What is the most well-known breed of dogs?

8. Who is Gang of Four's female member?

9. In what country was the AIDS virus first recognized?

10. What country has the biggest land area?

Quiz 67

1. Who wrote the Star Spangled Banner?

2. The boats of Christopher Columbus's original expedition are?

3. Where do the Super Bowl winning Cowboys come from?

4. Who discovered the penicillin?

5. What is the world's largest land animal?

6. What is the lion's name in *The Lion, The Witch and the Wardrobe?*

7. Is pawning the flag of the USA illegal?

8. What galaxy is Earth located in?

9. There are 300 bones in an infant and 206 bones in an adult: T/F?

10. Name the world's biggest island.

Quiz 68

1. What causes an Aurora?

2. By what Latin name was Rosa Gallica previously known?

3. What species has the Lane's Prince Albert, Wisley Crab, and May Queen?

4. Convert -40 degrees C to Fahrenheit?

5. What does the white dove symbolize?

6. Who is the gardener and author of Barnsdale Gardens?

7. Name the Celtic language spoken in Brittany.

8. What is the Milky Way?

9. What is Michael Phelps' number of golden wins at the 2008 Olympics?

10. Who was the Roman god of sleep?

Quiz 69

1. What is the common name for a cubic decimeter?

2. What does a fire need to keep it going?

3. What is the name of the garden included in the "Seven Wonders of the Ancient World?"

4. The colored part of an eye is called what?

5. Who are the four members of the Beatles?

6. In what street does the British Prime Minister live?

7. What is the biggest island in the world?

8. How many squares does a chess board have?

9. Beethoven composed how many symphonies?

10. What does bile do in your body?

Quiz 70

1. What is the Rio de Janeiro Mountain that overlooks its harbor?

2. Who are the Teenage Mutant Ninja Turtles?

3. What is the other name for a male bee?

4. Concientousness; Concientiousness; Concienciousness; Conscientiousness. Which is the correct spelling of the word meaning diligence?

5. What is Chopin's nationality?

6. Who is the first woman pilot to cross the Atlantic Ocean?

7. What is the world's largest bird?

8. Who has won more Oscars than anybody else?

9. What is the name of the main British military base in Afghanistan?

10. What is Basques' national game?

Quiz 71

1. A cow gives about how many glasses of milk in her lifetime?

2. Pompeii was destroyed in which year: AD79, 1079 or 2079?

3. The Australian city of Perth stands on what river?

4. Flounder is a character in which Disney movie?

5. Where can you find Earth's largest known meteorite crater?

6. Who was the first American President?

7. What city has the largest population?

8. In what bay is Alcatraz?

9. What is the codename for the planned German invasion of Britain?

10. What city is called the Windy City?

Quiz 72

1. The Olympic marathon was won twice in consecutive Olympic games by this athlete and this athlete only.

2. What is the prequel to the Lord of the Rings series?

3. What country is recognized as the "Country of Copper?"

4. What does the term piano mean?

5. Where would you find your pinna?

6. The new millennium started in which year?

7. What name is given to the official record of proceedings in Parliament?

8. Who played the undertaker in Dad's Army?

9. Who is the 1st president of the U.S.?

10. What do you call the highest pitched singing voice?

Quiz 73

1. What is UK TV's *Please Sir* school setting?

2. What is another word for a lexicon?

3. What color is the brandy liquor called Chartreuse?

4. What is the other name for a female bee?

5. What bird is the international symbol of happiness?

6. What is the only mammal that can fly?

7. Cars from Germany have these letters on them to show their country of origin.

8. What is the largest ocean on Earth?

9. What is the capital city of Spain?

10. What is the name of the policeman in Top Cat?

Quiz 74

1. What is the other name for a female swan?

2. Who is the actor of "*Papillion* and *The Great Escape*" who died in 1980?

3. What do the British call the American vegetable zucchini?

4. Battle of Bunker Hill was part of which war?

5. What is the black mineral used to make Victorian jewelry?

6. The earlier name of New York City was?

7. How many gold medals were the maximum won at an Olympics and whom were they won by?

8. Who is the inventor of the vacuum cleaner?

9. United States of America's largest state is?

10. What is the other name for a female fox?

Quiz 75

1. What is short for "binary digit"?

2. Who is both the F1 car world championship winner and motorbike champion of 2009?

3. What planet spins the slowest?

4. The U.S. fought itself in which war?

5. What country is the largest producer of rubber in the world?

6. Synonym's antonym is?

7. What does ATP stand for?

8. The decimal currency started being used by Britain in which year?

9. What river carries the maximum quantity of water into the sea?

10. From what tree do acorns come?

Quiz 76

1. What name is given to the 19th Century movement that is opposed to the mechanization within the textile industry?

2. From what language did the word "Ketchup" come from?

3. What is the longest river in the world?

4. What prized fungus do pigs dig around tree roots?

5. What is the world's oldest known city?

6. What is also known as The Tramp and The King of Comedy?

7. Julienne vegetables are cut how?

8. Who is the cop in the pre-school kid TV series *Balamory*?

9. What statue was pulled down in 1991 in Red Square?

10. Nostromo was the spaceship in which 1979 film?

Quiz 77

1. What sport does Constantino Rocca play?

2. What is the term for the part of the eye that has color?

3. What 1960s popular UK TV series featured a yellow lotus car?

4. The end of a rainbow has what, according to the myth?

5. What is the largest organ in the body?

6. What is the name given to George Washington's home and along what river did he live?

7. Who is the *I Married a Witch* film noir actress?

8. What is a Basilisk?

9. In football, where do the chargers come from?

10. In what English abbey would you find Poets Corner?

Quiz 78

1. Who wrote the Emancipation Proclamation?

2. What is the other name for a male horse?

3. What is the shipping line TV show set in Liverpool during 1800s?

4. Which sport features the free stroke, backstroke, and butterfly?

5. What country is home to the kangaroo?

6. At room temperature, what is the only metal that is liquid?

7. Who are the members of the Executive Branch?

8. How many degrees are found in a circle?

9. What Latin phrase means to excess to a sickening degree?

10. Why do things fall after you drop them?

Quiz 79

1. Where was Lope de Vega born?

2. What cocktail is made with vodka, Galliano, and OJ?

3. What do you call the planets outside our solar system?

4. What color is an absinthe?

5. How many members are there in the House of Representatives?

6. Who is the British general that was killed at Khartoum?

7. How many points does a compass have?

8. What country has the largest area of land?

9. Ring-a-ring O Roses nursery rhyme commemorates what historical event?

10. What is the principal export of Jamaica?

Quiz 80

1. The skull and the cross-bones flag were first flown by whose ship before the pirates?

2. How many curves are there in a paper clip?

3. "Russia is a riddle wrapped in a mystery inside an enigma," was first said by whom?

4. What four British cities have underground rail systems?

5. The left side or the right side of books have even number of pages. True or False?

6. What edible substance do bees make?

7. Gepetto, the woodcarver, carved what classic character?

8. What is a Yashmak?

9. What city is called the Big Apple?

10. What is the other name for a female bird?

Quiz 81

1. The world's oldest printed book that is still surviving is what?

2. In Japanese, what is the word for goodbye?

3. What country is the world's biggest producer of coffee?

4. What country ranks second in terms of land area?

5. What are the four sections in an orchestra?

6. What is the other name for a male goat?

7. Who wrote the Harry Potter series?

8. Air or water: sound travels faster in this.

9. Harry Potter is played by _____ in the film series.

10. How many sides does an octagon have?

Quiz 82

1. A firkin holds how many gallons of beer?

2. Who wrote the novel, David Copperfield?

3. Who is the politician that gave us the infamous Salmonella in Eggs scandal?

4. The Washington _____ are the U.S. NFL team for the state.

5. What name is given to the insect whose nymphs produce the frothed up plant sap recognized as cuckoo spit?

6. The initials *psso* mean what in knitting?

7. Who introduced pigs to North America?

8. What musical instrument did Pablo Casals play?

9. Which year gave birth to the public cinema?

10. Which country's volcano caused travel disruption in 2010?

Quiz 83

1. What is the name of the craft of knotting thread to create decorations that are handy?

2. Dover is the capital of what state?

3. UNO stands for?

4. Vest, beans, and quartet can all be preceded by what word and still make sense?

5. Once used as a type of currency, what type of bulbs once had value?

6. What state is called the Golden State?

7. A guitar's number of strings?

8. Australia's number of states that are an island?

9. 10/21/1805 saw this famous battle between the British and the French & Spanish Navies?

10. What is the highest recorded surface wind speed?

Quiz 84

1. In Kipling's Jungle Book, what kind of creature was Kaa?

2. In Canada, what is the NHL?

3. Who falls from a wall once he sat down (nursery rhyme)?

4. Whiskey and honey combined make what Scottish drink?

5. Shampoo and pajamas are terms that came from which country?

6. A frugivore eats a diet of what?

7. What is the name of Ewe's milk blue cheese?

8. Bjorn Borg won how many Wimbledon singles trophies?

9. What fictional character was also recognized as Lord Greystoke?

10. Roman Numerals does not contain what digit?

Quiz 85

1. Sir Walter Scott wrote what popular novel that features a hero who steals from the rich?

2. D.O.M. shows up on what French liqueur created in the 16th century?

3. What is the name of the blanket-like Mexican outerwear?

4. Give at least three colors from the Olympic flag.

5. What is the S.I unit of capacitance?

6. English prime minister's country residence is located in which county?

7. What is Xylem?

8. What are the great lakes of North America?

9. The Ordinance Survey publishes what sort of travel aid?

10. Where is the smallest bone in the body?

Quiz 86

1. This U.S. president had a type of doll name after him?

2. What is the symbol of iron?

3. What is the study of fossils?

4. What is removed from water in the process of desalination?

5. What are the four types of teeth?

6. The names of Italian mythological boys raised by wolves?

7. Volcano Vesuvius is located in?

8. The Sheffield Shield is competed for in what sport?

9. John F. Kennedy was assassinated by whom?

10. What is the Island of Cloves' common name?

Quiz 87

1. What is a bouquet garni?

2. Morlocks are creatures in which book series?

3. What has the highest mountain: Earth or Mars?

4. Is green at the top or bottom of a traffic light?

5. On TV, who did the character Lurch work for?

6. Who is the "Before He Cheats" singer-songwriter and American Idol winner?

7. In what English city is the Fitzwilliam Museum located?

8. What is the full name of the FBI?

9. What is a flat image that can be displayed in three dimensions?

10. What is the world's most widely spoken native tongue language?

Quiz 88

1. What company's logo is called the "swoosh"?

2. What British coin was also recognized as a bob?

3. What pigment do leaves get their green color?

4. What is the U.S. northernmost state?

5. How many years are there in a millennium?

6. What is the championship game called for the NFL?

7. A red circle on a white space is what country's flag?

8. What is *At first sight* legal term in Latin?

9. A live segment is featured in what Pixar movie?

10. The Sea of Tranquility is located where?

Quiz 89

1. What is the name of the gardens 10 miles outside of London near the River Thames?

2. In what year of the 20th century did three monarchs reign?

3. What is Switzerland financial center city's name?

4. When was the first chocolate bar became to be sold in every world market?

5. What is the year the Cold War end?

6. What is the name of the new villain in Iron Man 3: The Mandarin, The Marvellin or The Mandible?

7. Who is *The Silence of the Lambs* actress?

8. What is the solar system's hottest planet?

9. What unit of electrical power is equal to one joule per second?

10. What river passes through Madrid?

Quiz 90

1. The type of the blood is classified in what letters?

2. What type of grass do pandas eat?

3. Body temperature rises during digestion: T/F?

4. What is the largest of the Channel Islands?

5. The first atomic bomb was dropped when?

6. Who is England's soccer team's first black captain?

7. What is the Legislative Branch?

8. What continent is subjected to the world's largest ozone hole?

9. Who did Lady Diana Spencer marry?

10. What is the type of math that deals with shapes, angles, and their relationships?

Quiz 91

1. What is Sydney Blue Gum's scientific name?

2. A Neanderthal's brain is larger than a modern human's: T/F?

3. American, Rugby Union, Association (Soccer), or Australian: Which has the largest field size?

4. An adult has how many teeth, normally?

5. What flavor is Cointreau?

6. How many colors are there in a rainbow?

7. What is the first letter of the Greek alphabet?

8. Marlin, in the movie "Finding Nemo", is what fish?

9. Who is the first man to walk on the moon?

10. What color are Mickey Mouse's shorts?

Quiz 92

1. What is the red earthenware pottery's name?

2. What is the maiden name of the Queen mother?

3. How often are leap years?

4. Who is the Cubist movement creator?

5. Who is the Family Fortunes host after Monkhouse and prior to Dennis?

6. The Bronte sister's brother's name?

7. What country is Prague in?

8. In what decade was Madonna born?

9. What is converted into alcohol during brewing?

10. What is the Leaning Tower of Pisa's country?

Quiz 93

1. Frank Sinatra received a Best Supporting Actor Oscar in what 50s film?

2. What is a paintball pellet's max velocity (ft/sec): 50; 300; 1,000; or 3,000?

3. What is the closest U.S. State to Russia?

4. The moon's first man is aboard what spacecraft?

5. Kabul is the capital city of what country?

6. In what Park was the New York marathon run until 1970?

7. Marlon Brando was born in what decade of the century?

8. Andy receives what toy for his birthday in "Toy Story"?

9. What animal is Bullseye in Toy Story?

10. What is the largest state in the USA?

Quiz 94

1. What bone in the body is not joined to any other?

2. *Mad Max: Beyond The Thunderdome* singer who acted in the film?

3. Which is taller: the Statue of Liberty or the Eiffel Tower?

4. Lancelot Brown usually goes by what name?

5. The Theory of Relativity is made famous by?

6. Who wrote Lazarillo de Tormes?

7. Who are the members of the Judicial Branch?

8. How many members are there in the Senate?

9. A pipe and a box of tobacco were buried with whose 17th-century explorer?

10. P starts the name of this American state (only one)?

Quiz 95

1. When is the Independence Day of the United States?

2. What river flows through London?

3. What is the number of Great Lakes?

4. Who is Winston Churchill's successor in 1955?

5. The Mythological Nessie lives where?

6. Name the three types of rock.

7. Who is the first James Bond actor?

8. Who is the Diary of a Whimpy Kid's main character?

9. What is a Puffing Billy?

10. What is Chaucer's first name (Author of The Canterbury Tales)?

Quiz 96

1. What is classified by the ABO system?

2. What is the name of the world's highest waterfall?

3. What is Canada's national animal?

4. What company is owned by Bill Gates?

5. Name the three primary colors.

6. What is the name of the Greek mythological figure who stole fire from the gods?

7. When did Margaret Thatcher become the Prime Minister?

8. What sort of water creature is an oval pigtoe?

9. In the song, what street is Heartbreak Hotel located?

10. Basildon Bond spoof of James Bond is created by whom?

Quiz 97

1. What film fictionalized Persian Wars' Battle of Thermopylae?

2. Dr. Who has what anniversary to celebrate this year?

3. What country gifted Statute of Liberty to the U.S.?

4. Stars and Stripes is the nickname of the flag of what country?

5. The correctional facility for young adults in England is named after what village?

6. What is the symbol for Silver?

7. Whose speech "I have a Dream" belongs to?

8. The smallest bones in the human body are located where?

9. Two other rivers make up the River of Arabia. What are they?

10. What is the 6-letter Latin word that means "against?"

Quiz 98

1. Who is the singer recognized as the Swedish Nightingale?

2. Eurostar year of launch?

3. What is traditionally made by a Chandler?

4. The world's oldest dictionary is how old?

5. What is the largest ocean in the world?

6. What French term means the front of a building?

7. The human body's hardest substance is?

8. The Holy Grail is hiding, according to legend, in what musical city?

9. What is the distance around a circle called?

10. In needlework, what does UFO refer to?

Quiz 99

1. Gog and Magog were who in English mythology?

2. What is sushi traditionally wrapped in?

3. Om symbol represents which religion?

4. What country is the Taj Mahal located in?

5. The Beatles music band featured how many members?

6. The White Horse FA Cup Final occurred in what year?

7. What is a baby lion called?

8. How many planets are there in the solar system?

9. "Fasten your seatbelts. It's going to be a bumpy night," is said by whom in *All About Eve*?

10. What city hosted the 2012 Summer Olympic Games?

Quiz 100

1. What is the name of the Knipschildt luxury chocolate truffle?

2. The first public library in the U.S. was founded by whom?

3. What hills divide England from Scotland?

4. Mission, parent, script, late, fix, and fuse can share this one prefix and make 6 new words?

5. Who won the 2013 Superbowl?

6. Ascorbic acid's common name?

7. In what sport was Muhammad Ali the world champion?

8. What sport is the winner of the Harry Vardon trophy playing?

9. What city is called Sin City?

10. What is John Leach famous for making?

Answer Key

Quiz 1 Answers

1. Great Expectations
2. Felix Mendelssohn
3. George Carey
4. The 1980s
5. Nike
6. Sandals
7. Vatican City
8. MC
9. Pierre De Coubertin
10. John Adams

Quiz 2 Answers

1. Dried Plum
2. Photography
3. Tangled
4. Frankenstein
5. Baloo
6. 9
7. Sugar Rush.
8. Bitch
9. St. Patrick
10. A Midsummer Night's Dream

Quiz 3 Answers

1. John Steinbeck

2. Three

3. Robin (Batman And Robin)

4. Live And Let Die (1973)

5. Female (Tu-Whit) Then Male (Tu-Who)

6. 6

7. David Lloyd George

8. Robin Cousins

9. Fusion

10. Juke Box Jury

Quiz 4 Answers

1. The Mersey
2. Dimples
3. Fustanella
4. Hugh Laurie
5. 1912
6. Fiona
7. Roe
8. Tintagel
9. Bag Pipes
10. Pullet

Quiz 5 Answers

1. Yitzhak Rabin- Fifth Prime Minister of Israel

2. New York

3. England

4. Michael Palin

5. Mercury

6. The Great Barrier Reef, Australia

7. Paris

8. Iron Man

9. Giuseppe Garibaldi

10. Baseball

Quiz 6 Answers

1. Marilyn Monroe

2. Secret

3. The discrepancy in the two leg's strides may make people walk in circles.

4. Delaware

5. The Mona Lisa

6. AB Negative; <1% of the population

7. Binary

8. Books

9. A long tube of glass equipped with a stopcock that is commonly marked in 0.1ml units

10. Deciduous Trees

Quiz 7 Answers

1. Crinkley Bottom

2. Pisa

3. Orthodontist

4. Right

5. France

6. Greek

7. Andy Gibb

8. Around 120 Days

9. Egg Yolk

10. 6

Quiz 8 Answers

1. Hypoglycemia

2. Bishop

3. Walter Hunt

4. Katniss Everdeen

5. True

6. No Now Be Honest, Did You Try

7. De Lorean

8. Contour

9. Ovine

10. Saturn

Quiz 9 Answers

1. Louis Pasteur

2. Mr. Micawber (David Copperfield)

3. 27

4. Bouquet

5. Tinkerbell

6. George Bush

7. 4

8. Plymouth Argyle

9. Blondes

10. Scientology

Quiz 10 Answers

1. Bamboo

2. Bill Gates

3. Michelangelo, Donatello, Leonardo, Rafael

4. 4

5. South Africa

6. The branch that decides the meaning of laws, how they are applied, and interprets laws based on the Constitution.

7. Bull

8. Manslaughter

9. Helen Dunmore

10. Bodleian

Quiz 11 Answers

1. Washington DC, District Of Columbia

2. Humphry Davy

3. Moss

4. One Pound Coin

5. Greek X which means Christ

6. Marlin

7. Eric Clapton

8. Bric A Brac

9. Simon Templar

10.   Hovercraft

Quiz 12 Answers

1. China

2. Toby

3. May

4. 5

5. Sugar Cane

6. Frank Whittle

7. Frederic Chopin

8. 13

9. Shrek

10. Canada

Quiz 13 Answers

1. Jamaica

2. Buddy Holly

3. Big Ben

4. Cerebrovascular Accident

5. Rowan

6. Czechoslovakia & USA

7. Peter Piper

8. Russell Watson

9. 50 Inches

10. David Copperfield

Quiz 14 Answers

1. A pillow.

2. 100,000 Atmospheres and 3000 degrees Celsius

3. Dom Perignon

4. Hippopotamus

5. Fawn

6. Birmingham

7. The Lake District

8. Hammer Horror

9. Jerusalem

10. Guernica

Quiz 15 Answers

1. Alexander Graham Bell

2. About 360,000 to 405,000 kilometers

3. 12

4. 37

5. Benthos

6. A Mackintosh

7. Korea

8. A form of medicine in ancient times where holes are made in the skull.

9. Holt

10. Beards

Quiz 16 Answers

1. Paul McCartney and Ringo Starr

2. United States Library of Congress, Washington Dc

3. Flowerpot Men

4. 4

5. Sleeping

6. Yellow and Bird

7. Hard Black

8. Eastenders

9. Sir George Everest

10. China

Quiz 17 Answers

1. Knight

2. Hanukkah

3. Boomerang

4. 1932

5. Fry, Fingerlings

6. The Pressure Of A Closed System

7. Doe

8. Speed (From Greek Takhus, Swift)

9. Ibiza

10. First 10 amendments (additions) to the US Constitution

Quiz 18 Answers

1. Billion

2. Aloo

3. The Piano

4. Cancer

5. The Eye

6. River Aire

7. Edwin Land

8. About 8 minutes and 18 seconds

9. A Half

10.   Peter Beardsley

Quiz 19 Answers

1. Maria Estela Isabel Peron

2. Dugout

3. Igraine

4. Mark Zuckerberg

5. Heart

6. Napoleon Bonaparte

7. About 45 million years old

8. 986 degrees Fahrenheit

9. Blue-Green Algae

10. World Cup

Quiz 20 Answers

1. India

2. Acupuncture

3. Box

4. Webbed

5. The Heat Of Chilies

6. September, April, June, November

7. Washing Machine

8. New Zealand

9. California's Bristlecone Pine

10. Count Alessandro Volta

Quiz 21 Answers

1. Africa, Australia, Antarctica, Europe, Asia, South America, and North America

2. 14

3. Theodore Roosevelt

4. Abraham Lincoln

5. Egypt

6. Red, Yellow, Blue

7. Miner's Safety Lamp, The Davy Lamp

8. A Fruit

9. The Man Of Steel

10. Locomotion No. 1

Quiz 22 Answers

1. Jackson Pollack

2. Kiki Dee

3. Roller Skates

4. Peter Jackson

5. Red

6. Alarm Clock

7. Canada And Mexico

8. Cockerel

9. 0, 1, 1, 2, 3, 5, 8, 13, 21

10. Rudolf Nureyev

Quiz 23 Answers

1. 9
2. Venus
3. Blue
4. 10
5. Daintree Forest North Of Cairns, Australia
6. Rice Krispies
7. Duck-Billed Platypus
8. A Substance That Causes Fever
9. Van Pelt
10. Ice

Quiz 24 Answers

1. Goal Keeper

2. Billy Bunter

3. Los Angeles

4. Jacqueline Wilson

5. A Kid

6. George Eastman

7. 70% hydrogen and 28% helium by mass. Everything else amounts to less than 2%.

8. Gold

9. The pH Scale

10. Gk Chesterton

Quiz 25 Answers

1. 6

2. 1000

3. 300

4. Griffin

5. Calorie

6. 6

7. Sovereign

8. Bob Marley

9. Magnetism

10. White Blood Cells, or Leukocytes

Quiz 26 Answers

1. Anton Chekov

2. Yellow

3. Happiness

4. 5

5. Sherlock Holmes

6. Adrian Mole

7. Jana Novotna

8. Blue

9. Bowls

10. Eurostar

Quiz 27 Answers

1. Toyota

2. Pen

3. Johannes Chrysostomus Wolfgangus Theophilus Mozart

4. Poseidon

5. Nanny

6. May

7. Earth

8. Gnomon

9. 300 (13+17+19+23+29+31+37+41+43+47=300)

10. 8

Quiz 28 Answers

1. Volleyball uses techniques called spiking and blocking

2. India

3. JR Tolkien

4. Martina Navratilova (1982-87, Also 1978, 79, 90)

5. Arizona

6. Lake Superior

7. Theodore Roosevelt 42

8. 4

9. A three-Headed dog that guards the gates of the Underworld

10. 0 And 1

Quiz 29 Answers

1. 1986

2. Spain

3. Ireland

4. Yellow

5. Australia

6. Kit

7. Herd Or Drove

8. A Farrier

9. Water

10. Jackie Robinson

Quiz 30 Answers

1. ITv News At Ten

2. Lizard Point

3. Egg, Larva, Pupa

4. Uranus

5. Casablanca

6. Franklin D. Roosevelt

7. Insulin

8. The Congress - The Senate and The House Of Representatives

9. France

10. Jupiter

Quiz 31 Answers

1. V

2. Cardiff

3. Blofeld (Ernst Stavro)

4. Table Tennis

5. Texas

6. Tony Curtis

7. True – up to 70%!

8. Approximately 60%

9. Superior, Michigan, Huron, Erie, And Ontario

10. Charles Macintosh

Quiz 32 Answers

1. Dominicans
2. Id
3. Grumpy, Sleepy, Happy, Sneezy, Doc, Bashful, and Dopey
4. English Channel
5. Rabbits
6. 100°C
7. Chick, Hatchling
8. Bubonic Plague
9. False
10. 300

Quiz 33 Answers

1. 1st January 1999

2. Arthur

3. Buffalo

4. 50

5. 1960 (19Th February)

6. Goat

7. Debussy

8. Fred Flintstone

9. Anne Rice

10. Mr. Spock (Star Trek)

Quiz 34 Answers

1. A pumpkin

2. Colin Chapman

3. Calf

4. Smelting

5. Ganges Delta

6. Kenya

7. The Ladies Mercury

8. Double Eagle (Albatross)

9. Around 376 600 km away

10. Bel Air

Quiz 35 Answers

1. Narcissus

2. Excalibur

3. Waterloo

4. Pinocchio

5. Middle

6. Skegness (1936)

7. Yellow

8. 1093

9. Mountains in Scotland

10. Ewe

Quiz 36 Answers

1. 8,000 Miles
2. Tercel
3. Tom
4. Iron Man
5. Madagascar
6. Galileo
7. George
8. Gander
9. A Sword
10. Cyprus

Quiz 37 Answers

1. Led Zeppelin
2. Granada Spain
3. Nick Griffin
4. Emily Davison
5. 12
6. Henry 8Th
7. Texas
8. The African Queen (Humphrey Bogart & Katherine Hepburn)
9. Four Years
10. Paint Your Wagon

Quiz 38 Answers

1. Ram

2. Gold

3. Thailand

4. Mercury

5. Mare

6. Elephant

7. Grant

8. Switzerland

9. San Francisco

10. The name "Coyote" means trickster

Quiz 39 Answers

1. Beauty and the Beast

2. 1,300 meters

3. Bailey

4. El Caudillo

5. Jack (and the Beanstalk)

6. Declaration of Independence

7. Hatchling

8. Jugged Hare

9. Tweed

10. Dog

Quiz 40 Answers

1. A mythical beast that typically have the body of a lion, sting of a scorpion, and the face of a man
2. Cheetah
3. Hydrogen
4. Eaglet
5. Millennium
6. Roberto Baggio
7. 13,000
8. Alexander Eiffel
9. Agincourt
10. Sunny

Quiz 41 Answers

1. Refugees

2. Groucho, Zeppo, Harpo, And Chico

3. Tchaikovsky

4. Ian Fleming

5. Bear

6. April 23, 1564

7. A book in digital form

8. Lily

9. Lamb

10. Belmont

Quiz 42 Answers

1. Abraham Lincoln

2. Right

3. Tom, Dick, Harry

4. Peach

5. Eric Schmidt

6. Single Lens Reflex

7. 1,000

8. Riverside (Chester-Le-Street, Durham)

9. Antiques Roadshow

10. Honolulu

Quiz 43 Answers

1. Yes, under zero gravity, the spine's cartilage expands

2. Dragon

3. Oakland

4. Steam

5. Coins (And/or Medals)

6. 13

7. Birkenhead

8. Captain Nemo

9. Idaho

10. About 5 billion years

Quiz 44 Answers

1. 3
2. Mike Tindall
3. 7
4. Serena
5. Venice
6. St. Luke
7. Sherlock Holmes
8. 6
9. 1978
10. 6

Quiz 45 Answers

1. London

2. Internal Revenue Service

3. US Open

4. Wine

5. A Giraffe

6. 22nd Amendment

7. Mortimer Mouse

8. A Neutron Star

9. Red, Yellow, and Blue

10. Florence Nightingale

Quiz 46 Answers

1. Nadia Comaneci

2. Ford

3. TRUE

4. Ophthalmoscope

5. Queen Elizabeth II (just beat Queen Victoria on Sept 9, 2015)

6. Golf

7. 1616

8. George

9. The branch that carries out/enforces laws

10. Shep

Quiz 47 Answers

1. Gregory Peck (Captain Ahab)

2. Coastal Area Of Dead Sea

3. False: They hosted in 1960

4. Shredded Wheat

5. Piccolo

6. From dogs

7. Mt. Everest

8. England

9. 366

10. Japan

Quiz 48 Answers

1. Femur

2. A word that is the opposite of another word

3. Turkey

4. 1914

5. Print On Demand

6. Because the lens of the eyes are still growing, becoming less transparent, and thicker

7. The Supreme Court

8. Peanut

9. K, M

10. Meteorite

Quiz 49 Answers

1. The Merchant of Venice

2. Atlantic Ocean

3. Airplane

4. World War II

5. Tadpole, Polliwog

6. Red

7. Apollo

8. Montague & Capulet

9. Three

10. Snowdrops

Quiz 50 Answers

1. In the year 1867

2. 5

3. Black And White

4. Mercury

5. Apple

6. Jack Nicklaus

7. The White House

8. Spider-Man

9. Basil

10. 1939

Quiz 51 Answers

1. Monaco

2. Dracula

3. Pink

4. Fortune Telling

5. Electoral College

6. Spare

7. 1600 Pennsylvania Ave NW, Washington, Dc 20500

8. Whitney Houston

9. The Black Mamba

10. A, B, AB, and O

Quiz 52 Answers

1. Mount Kilimanjaro

2. Greece

3. South America

4. 12

5. Middle finger

6. Rocky Marciano

7. Albatross

8. Pimento

9. Ganymede

10. The number of protons in it

Quiz 53 Answers

1. Menelaus

2. Five

3. Richard Rogers

4. Nutmeg

5. Trans-Canada

6. 3

7. Apostrophes

8. True. It dilates blood vessels

9. Gold

10. Nancy Astor

Quiz 54 Answers

1. Cow

2. Book

3. Esperanto

4. Honey

5. The energy of the universe remains constant

6. Sleeping Beauty

7. Rugby Union

8. A spear

9. Kenny Everett

10. Brazil

Quiz 55 Answers

1. Dante Gabriel Rossetti

2. A Joey

3. James Cook

4. China

5. Frass

6. Great Britain

7. Knee (It's the kneecap)

8. Ice

9. Anne Nightingale

10. NBA Finals

Quiz 56 Answers

1. Goose

2. 3

3. Education

4. China Clay

5. Jamaica

6. Shakespeare

7. Ten

8. Cock

9. Norway

10. Yes

Quiz 57 Answers

1. A tie

2. Mt. Everest

3. Australia

4. Between Spain and France

5. Liffey

6. Bashful

7. 1967

8. Mary Magdalene

9. Argentinian

10. The Capital Building

Quiz 58 Answers

1. Déjà Vu

2. 16th April 1746

3. Pride

4. Proxima Centauri

5. Michelangelo

6. Herring

7. Drake

8. Portuguese

9. Gosling

10. Lorraine Chase

Quiz 59 Answers

1. 1900

2. Hawaii

3. Egypt

4. Stag Or Buck

5. Parker

6. 1960

7. Tantalus

8. Coventry

9. BBC

10. 18

Quiz 60 Answers

1. Cauliflower Soup

2. Barack Obama

3. Hedwig

4. Leonardo Da Vinci

5. In the year 1912

6. Antimatter

7. The thymus gland or pancreas of an animal (food)

8. 16

9. Freedom For The Slaves

10. Pennsylvania

Quiz 61 Answers

1. New Zealand

2. 6

3. Promenade Concerts

4. Panther

5. Baked Alaska

6. Sherlock Holmes

7. Sleep

8. February

9. Orange

10. From a star

Quiz 62 Answers

1. Up to 75,000 flowers

2. 8

3. Egypt

4. Dubai

5. Kidney

6. Cygnet Or Flapper

7. Ascorbic Acid is the other name for Vitamin C

8. Lose their leaves in winter

9. Spreadsheet

10. A legendary sea monster off the coast of Norway causing large whirlpools

Quiz 63 Answers

1. Marion Morrison

2. Camels

3. Thomas Edison

4. 30

5. John

6. John Wayne

7. Anniversary (typically of a parent's death)

8. Friar Tuck

9. Woody

10. Baggins

Quiz 64 Answers

1. Black Beauty

2. Scalene

3. Thomas Mann

4. Let the buyer beware

5. Lettuce

6. 5

7. Washington Post

8. Big Top

9. Bannockburn

10. Steel

Quiz 65 Answers

1. Sahara Desert

2. Margaret Thatcher

3. Top of the pops

4. No. It is an alloy of a white metal and gold

5. The Becquerel (Bq) 1 Bq = 1 disintegration per second

6. Broomstick

7. Lungs

8. Arizona

9. Calf

10. 15-20 million years old

Quiz 66 Answers

1. 5

2. Jezebel

3. Jackie Robinson

4. Kryptonite

5. Alabama (Or Michigan)

6. Mah-Jong

7. Retriever

8. Shirley Williams (SDP = Social Democratic Party)

9. USA

10. Russia

Quiz 67 Answers

1. Francis Scott-Key

2. Niña, Pinta, Santa Maria

3. Dallas

4. Fleming

5. Elephant

6. Aslan

7. True

8. The Milky Way

9. True

10. Greenland

Quiz 68 Answers

1. Charged particles from the solar wind

2. Rosa Mundi

3. Apples

4. -40

5. Peace

6. Geoff Hamilton

7. Breton

8. Spiral Galaxy

9. Eight

10. Somnus

Quiz 69 Answers

1. Liter

2. Oxygen

3. The Hanging Gardens Of Babylon

4. The Iris

5. John Lennon, Ringo Starr, Paul Mccartney, George Harrison

6. Downing Street (Number 10)

7. Greenland

8. 64

9. 9

10. Emulsify fats in the small intestine

Quiz 70 Answers

1. Sugar Loaf

2. Donatello, Leonardo, Raphael, and Michael Angelo

3. Drone

4. Conscientiousness

5. Polish

6. Amelia Earheart

7. The Ostrich

8. Walt Disney

9. Camp Bastion

10. Pelota

Quiz 71 Answers

1. 200,000

2. Mount Vesuvius

3. Swan River

4. The Little Mermaid

5. Vredefort Ring in South Africa. 299km diameter!

6. George Washington

7. Tokyo

8. San Francisco Bay

9. Operation Sea lion

10. Chicago

Quiz 72 Answers

1. Abebe Bikila

2. The Hobbit

3. Zambia

4. To be played softly

5. The outer ear

6. The year 2000

7. Hansard

8. John Laurie

9. George Washington

10. Soprano is the highest pitch

Quiz 73 Answers

1. Fenn Street

2. Dictionary

3. Green or yellow

4. Worker or Queen

5. Bluebird

6. The Bat

7. D

8. Pacific

9. Madrid

10. Officer Dibble

Quiz 74 Answers

1. Cob

2. Steve McQueen

3. Courgettes

4. American War Of Independence

5. Jet

6. New Amsterdam

7. Michael Phelps

8. Huber Booth

9. Alaska

10. Vixen

Quiz 75 Answers

1. Bit

2. John Surtees

3. Venus

4. The Civil War

5. Malaysia

6. Of course, it is antonym itself!

7. Adenosine Triphosphate

8. 1971

9. Amazon River

10. Oak

Quiz 76 Answers

1. Luddites

2. Chinese

3. Nile River

4. Truffles

5. Damascus (Syria)

6. Charlie Chaplin

7. Thin Strips (Or Shreds Or Sliced Lengthways)

8. Pc Plum

9. Lenin's

10. Alien

Quiz 77 Answers

1. Golf

2. Iris

3. The Prisoner

4. Pot Of Gold

5. Skin

6. Mt. Vernon/Potomac River

7. Veronica Lake

8. A creature, like a lizard, serpent or dragon, that kills with its looks or breath

9. San Diego

10. Westminster

Quiz 78 Answers

1. Abraham Lincoln

2. Stallion Or Stud

3. The One in Line

4. Swimming

5. Australia

6. Mercury

7. The President, the Vice President, the Cabinet

8. 360

9. Ad Nauseam

10. Gravity

Quiz 79 Answers

1. Madrid

2. Harvey Wallbanger

3. Extrasolar Planets

4. Green

5. 425 members, number per state based on the population of the state

6. Charles Gordon

7. 32

8. Russia

9. The Great Plague Of 1665

10. Sugar

Quiz 80 Answers

1. Knights Templar

2. 3

3. Winston Churchill

4. Liverpool, Glasgow, Newcastle, and London

5. Left

6. Honey

7. Pinocchio

8. An Arab Veil

9. New York City

10. Hen

Quiz 81 Answers

1. The Diamond Sutra

2. Sayonara

3. Brazil

4. Canada

5. String, Brass, Woodwind, Percussion

6. Billy

7. JK Rowling

8. Water

9. Daniel Radcliffe

10. 8

Quiz 82 Answers

1. Nine

2. Charles Dickens

3. Edwina Currie

4. Redskins

5. Froghopper

6. Pass Slipped Stitch Over

7. Christopher Columbus

8. Cello

9. 1896

10. Iceland

Quiz 83 Answers

1. Macramé

2. Delaware

3. United Nations Organization

4. String

5. Tulips

6. California

7. 6

8. Tasmania

9. Battle Of Trafalgar

10. 372Km/H.

Quiz 84 Answers

1. Snake

2. National Hockey League

3. Humpty Dumpty

4. Drambuie

5. India

6. A frugivore is a fruit eater

7. Roquefort

8. Five

9. Tarzan

10. 0 (Zero)

Quiz 85 Answers

1. Ivanhoe

2. Benedictine

3. Poncho

4. Blue, Red, Green, Yellow, and Black

5. Farad

6. Buckinghamshire

7. The plant's tissue that is hollow and woody which carries minerals and water to the entire plant.

8. Lake Ontario, Lake Erie, Lake Huron, Lake Superior, Lake Michigan

9. Maps

10. Ear

Quiz 86 Answers

1. Theodore Roosevelt

2. Fe

3. Paleontology

4. Salt

5. Molars, pre-molars, incisors, and canines

6. Romulus And Remus

7. Italy

8. Cricket (Australia)

9. Lee Harvey Oswald

10. Madagascar

Quiz 87 Answers

1. Bunch of herbs used to add flavor to food

2. The time machine

3. Mars

4. Bottom

5. Addams Family

6. Carrie Underwood

7. Cambridge

8. Federal Bureau Of Investigation

9. Hologram

10. Mandarin Chinese

Quiz 88 Answers

1. Nike
2. Shilling
3. Chlorophyll
4. Alaska
5. 1000
6. Super Bowl
7. Japan
8. Prima Facie
9. Wall-E
10. The Moon

Quiz 89 Answers

1. Kew Gardens

2. 1936

3. Zurich

4. KitKat

5. 1989

6. The Mandarin

7. Jodie Foster

8. Venus, surface temperature 4600°c

9. The Watt

10. Manzanares

Quiz 90 Answers

1. A, B, and O

2. Bamboo

3. True

4. Jersey

5. It was dropped on August 6, 1945

6. Paul Ince

7. The branch that comes up/makes all the laws

8. Antarctica

9. Prince Charles

10. Trigonometry

Quiz 91 Answers

1. Eucalyptus Saligna

2. True

3. Australian

4. 32

5. Orange

6. 7

7. Alpha

8. A Clownfish

9. Neil Armstrong, in 1969

10. Red

Quiz 92 Answers

1. Terracotta

2. Bowes-Lyon

3. Every 4 years

4. Pablo Picasso

5. Max Bygraves

6. Branwell

7. Czech Republic

8. The 1950s

9. Sugar

10. Italy

Quiz 93 Answers

1. From here to eternity

2. 300

3. Alaska

4. Apollo 11

5. Afghanistan

6. Central Park

7. The 1920s

8. Buzz Lightyear

9. Horse

10. Alaska

Quiz 94 Answers

1. Hyoid Bone

2. Tina Turner

3. The Eiffel Tower

4. Capability Brown

5. Albert Einstein

6. Anonymous

7. The Supreme Court And The Lower Courts

8. 100 members total, two from each state, 6-year term if not re-elected

9. Sir Walter Raleigh

10. Pennsylvania

Quiz 95 Answers

1. July 4th (Originally 1776)

2. The Thames

3. 5

4. Sir Robert Anthony Eden

5. Ans Loch Ness

6. Igneous, Sedimentary, and Metamorphic

7. Sir Sean Connery

8. Greg Heffley

9. Steam Train

10. Geoffrey

Quiz 96 Answers

1. Blood systems

2. Angel Falls in Venezuela

3. Beaver

4. Microsoft

5. Red, blue, and yellow

6. Prometheus

7. 1979

8. A kind of freshwater mussel

9. Lonely Street

10. Russ Abbott

Quiz 97 Answers

1. 300

2. 50th anniversary

3. France

4. United States Of America

5. Borstal

6. Ag

7. Martin Luther King, Jr.

8. What Are They Called

9. Tigris And Euphrates

10. Versus

Quiz 98 Answers

1. Jenny Lind

2. November 14, 1994

3. Candles

4. Existed since 2300 BC

5. The Pacific Ocean

6. Facade

7. Tooth Enamel

8. Glastonbury (Somerset, UK)

9. Circumference

10. An unfinished item

Quiz 99 Answers

1. Giants

2. Edible seaweed

3. Hinduism

4. India

5. 4

6. 1923

7. Cub

8. 8

9. Bette Davis (As Margo Channing)

10. London

Quiz 100 Answers

1. Chocopologie

2. Benjamin Franklin

3. Cheviots

4. Trans

5. Baltimore Ravens

6. Vitamin C

7. Boxing

8. Golf

9. Las Vegas

10. Pottery

Made in the USA
San Bernardino, CA
12 November 2018